JUST IMAGINE!

7 Elementary Piano Solos That Encourage Expressive, Imaginative Playing

MARTHA MIER

Contents

Foreword

A piano student will perform music with more expression and feeling when able to see or imagine a mental image of what the music is about.

Just Imagine! Book 1 contains seven solos which help the student feel the mood of the music. "Chinese Water Lilies" paints a picture of quiet, peaceful serenity, while the playful antics of "The Jolly Clown" call for a scherzo-like interpretation. A student might imagine being in a deep, dark forest on a moonlit night while playing the mysterious sounds of "Little Gray Owl."

Try the wings of your imagination, and enjoy the variety of moods, color and style found in Just Imagine!

Martha Mier

Artwork: Liana Kelley
Cover Design: Lisa Barrett & Ruth McKinney
Music Engraving: Thomas Schaller

Sunflower Boogie

Brightly

Martha Mier

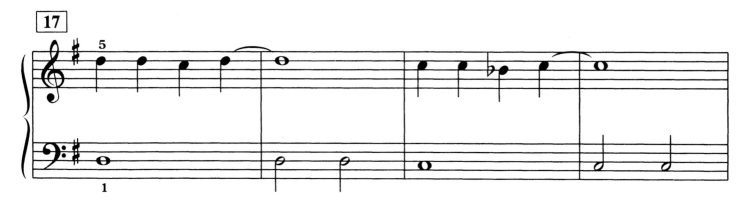

4

Chinese Water Lilies

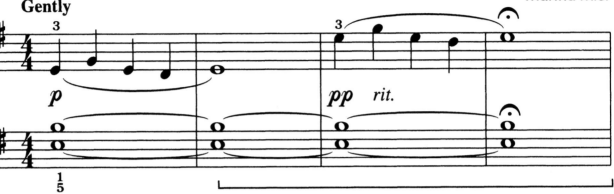

Martha Mier

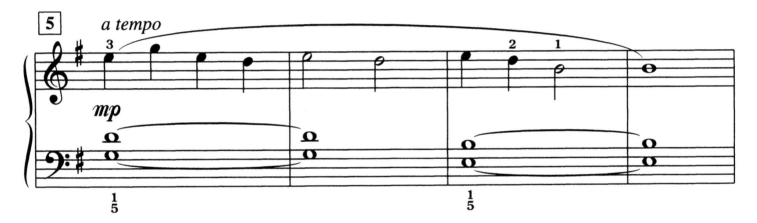

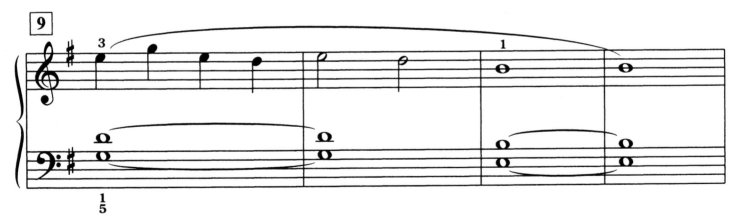

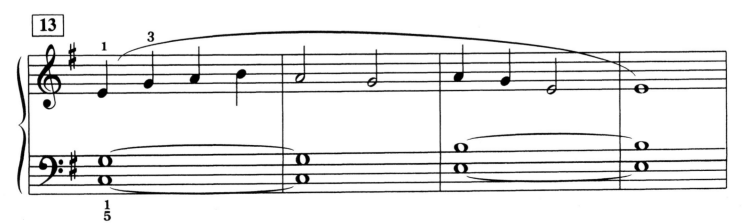

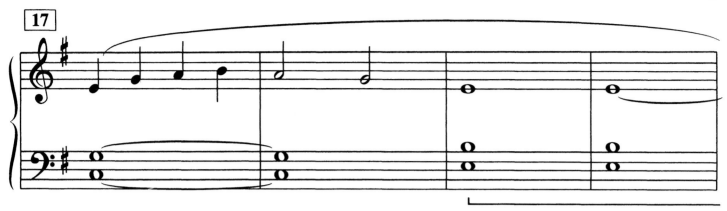

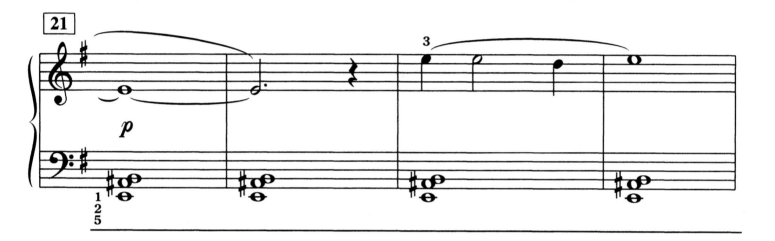

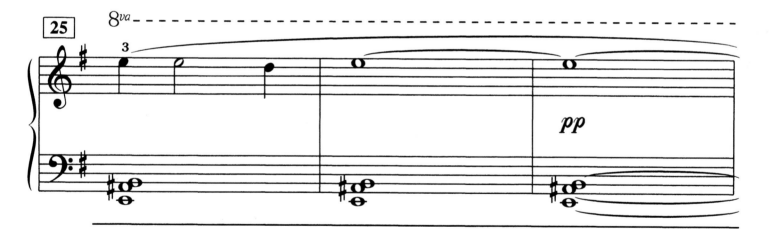

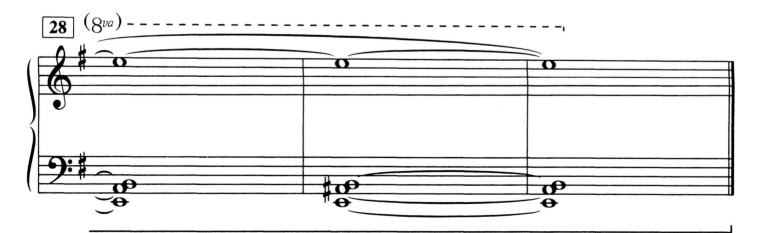

Little Gray Owl

Mysteriously

Martha Mier

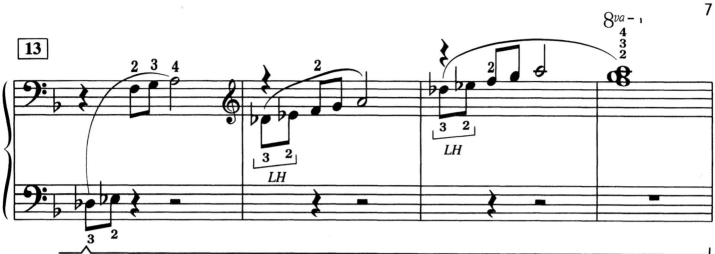

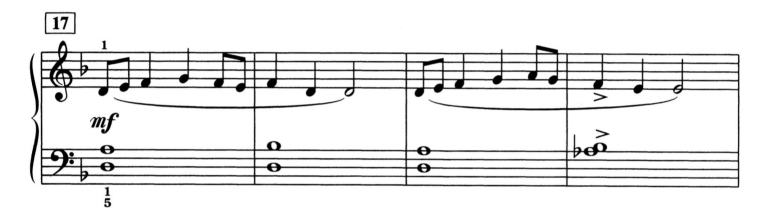

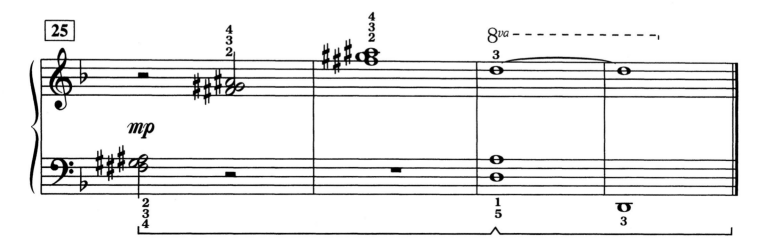

Rain Dance

Martha Mier

With a steady beat

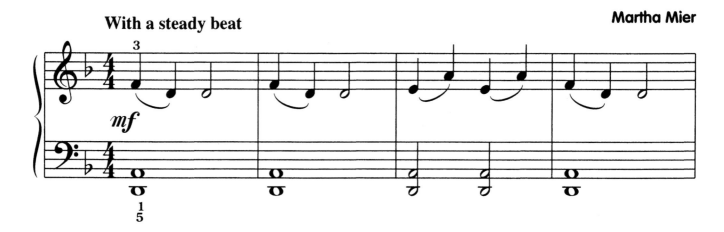

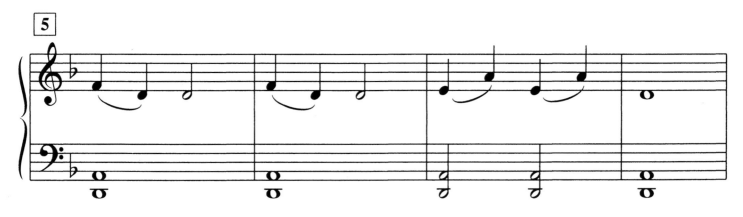

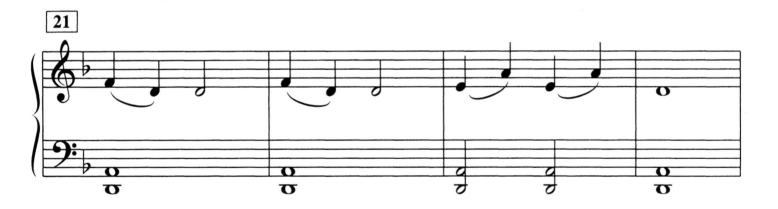

The Jolly Clown

Cheerfully

Martha Mier

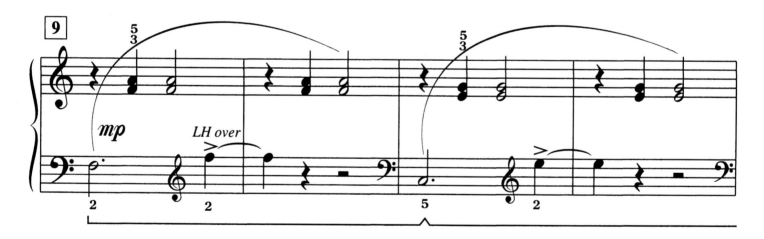

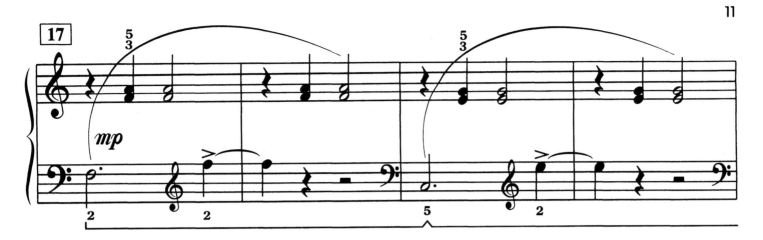

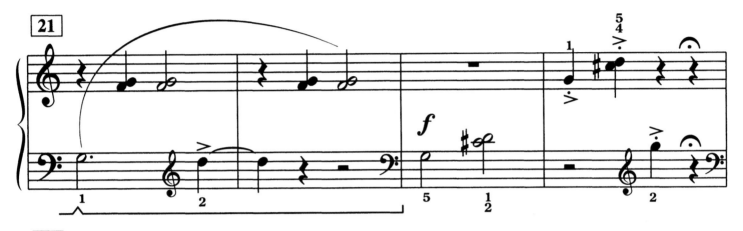

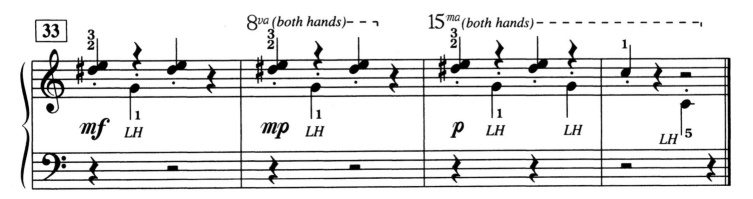

Clogging Dance

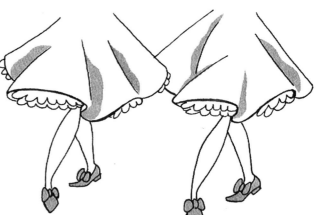

Martha Mier

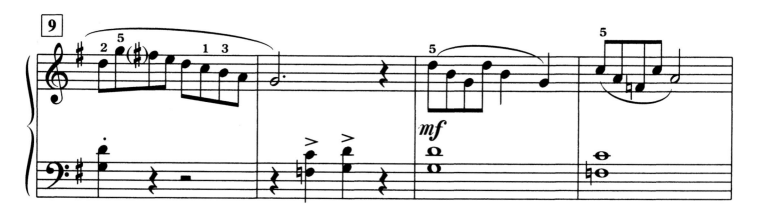

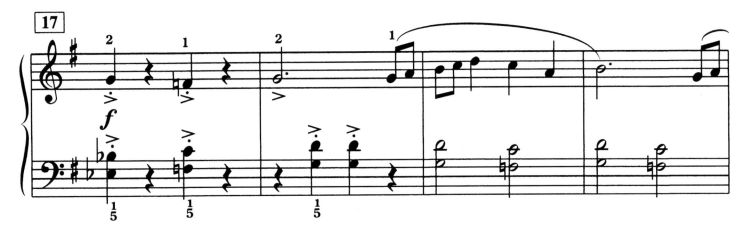

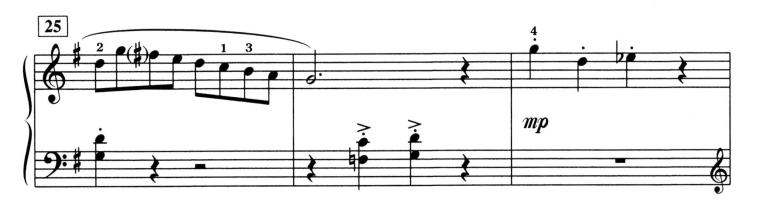

Lady Bug Waltz

Martha Mier

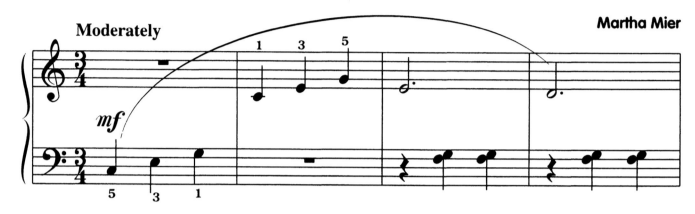

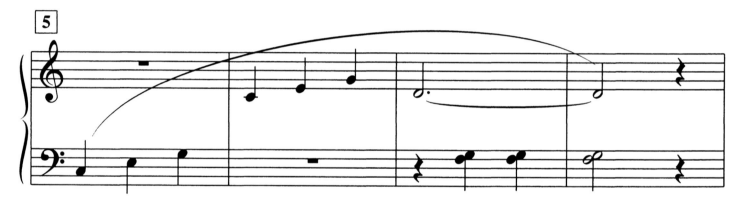

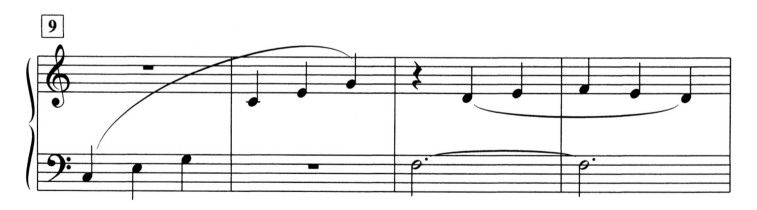

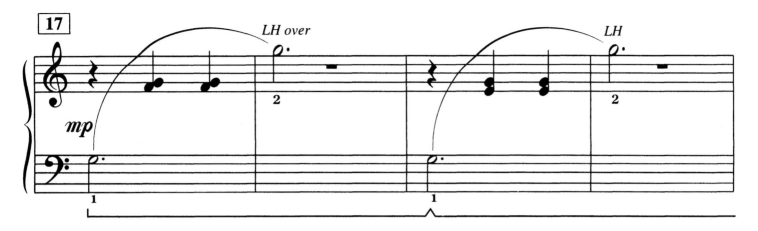

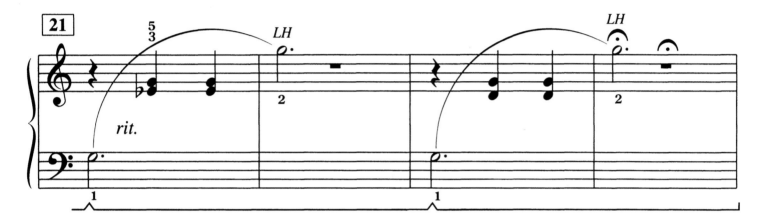

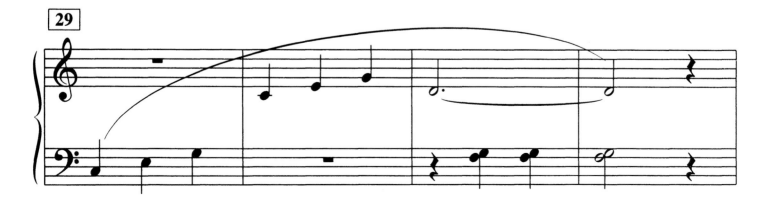

33

37

41
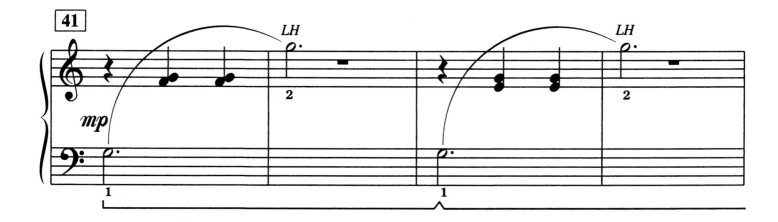

45
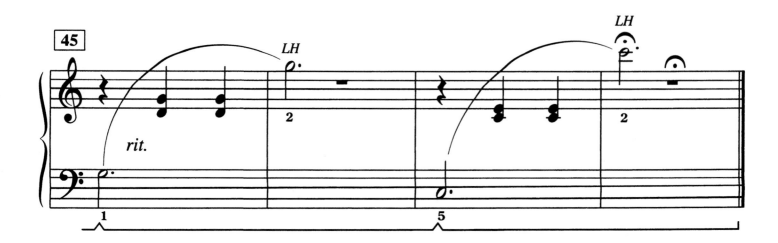